HEINEMANN
STATE STUDIES

Uniquely Nebraska

Jamie Stockman Opat

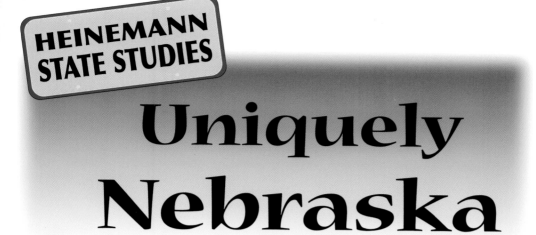

Heinemann Library
Chicago, Illinois

Designed by Heinemann Library
Printed in China by WKT Company Limited.

08 07 06 05 04
10 9 8 7 6 5 4 3 2 1

**Library of Congress
Cataloging-in-Publication Data**

Stockman Opat, Jamie.
  Uniquely Nebraska / Jamie Stockman Opat.
    p. cm. -- (Heinemann state studies)
Includes bibliographical references and index.
  ISBN 1-4034-4649-0 (lib. bdg.) --
ISBN 1-4034-4718-7 (pbk.)
  1. Nebraska -- Juvenile literature. [1. Nebraska.]
I. Title. II. Series.
  F666.3.S76 2004
  978.2--dc22

                           2003025717

Acknowledgments

Development and photo research by
BOOK BUILDERS LLC

The author and publishers are grateful to the
following for permission to reproduce copyrighted
material:

Cover photographs by (top, L-R): Tom Bean/
Corbis; Corbis; Joe Sohm/Alamy; Corbis; (main):
David Muench/Corbis

Title page (L-R): Alamy; Mike Whye; Contents
page: Mike Whye; p. 3, p. 6 Corbis; p. 5, 9, 19,
21, 25, 26, 29, 31, 36, 43 Mike Whye; p. 7 Tom
Bean/Corbis; p. 8, 44, 45 maps by IMA for BOOK
BUILDERS LLC; p. 10 Courtesy Dan Nitzel; p. 11
Center student photo taken at Edgerton Explorit,
Aurora, NE (www.edgerton.org); p. 12 Courtesy
Kraft Foods; p. 13 T Joe Sohm/Alamy; p. 13B One
Mile Up; p. 15T, 15B, 23, 33, 40 Alamy; p. 16T, 18
Courtesy Broken Arrow Wilderness; p. 16B
Courtesy of Robert W. Hines/USFW; p. 17T
Courtesy of ARS/USDA; p. 17B Courtesy Steve
Brusatte; p.22, 24T, 24B Hulton/Getty; p. 27
Courtesy Boys Town Hall of History Collection; p.
28 Courtesy Lincoln Chamber of Commerce; p. 30
Courtesy Nebraska Supreme Court Information
and Education Office; p. 31T Courtesy George
Hipple; p. 32B Larry Cook; p. 34 B.
Minton/Heinemann Library; p. 35 R.
Capozzelli/Heinemann Library; p. 37 Brian
Bahr/Getty Images; p. 38 T Al Bello/Getty Images;
p. 38B Courtesy Creighton Athletics; p. 41 AP/Bob
Bailie; p. 42 Courtesy © Erik
Stenbakken/stembakken.com; p. 44 David
Muench/Corbis

Special thanks to William McKane of the University
of Nebraska for his expert comments in the
preparation of this book.

Every effort has been made to contact copyright
holders of any material reproduced in this book.
Any omissions will be rectified in subsequent
printings if notice is given to the publisher.

Cover Pictures

Top (left to right) Nebraska state flag,
Omaha, Badlands, corn field **Main** Chimney
Rock National Historical Site

Some words are shown in bold, **like this.**
You can find out what they mean by looking
in the glossary.

Contents

Uniquely Nebraska

Nebraska is a patchwork landscape of colorful corn and soybean fields, **native** prairie grasses, and rolling rivers. Nebraska offers many unique—or one of a kind—reminders of U.S. history. Along Highway 8, near the Little Blue River, one can see wagon tracks made 150 years ago as settlers journeyed through Nebraska on the 2,000-mile Oregon Trail that leads from Missouri to Oregon. Fort Robinson, near Crawford, is a historic military post established in 1877 to keep peace among settlers and Native Americans.

Nebraska is nestled in the midwestern region of the United States. It is bordered by six states: Colorado, Wyoming, South Dakota, Iowa, Missouri, and Kansas.

ORIGIN OF THE STATE'S NAME

Nebraska's name comes from the Native American word *nebrathka,* or "flat water." The Oto and Omaha peoples used this word to describe the wide and shallow Platte River, which runs from west to east across the state. The Platte River Valley is important to Nebraska's history. It served as a transportation route for pioneers traveling to Oregon, California, and Utah in the mid-1800s.

Omaha serves as the center of industry for eastern Nebraska and western Iowa.

Toadstool Geologic Park

About 30 million years ago fast-flowing rivers gave Toadstool Geologic Park, near Crawford in northwest Nebraska, its uniquely shaped rock formations. The formations look like giant stone toadstools. The rivers deposited coarse-grained sand in the riverbed and silt, or fine soil, along the banks. Layers of sandstone and siltstone  pressed together as the rivers changed course again and again. As the siltstone **eroded,** the sandstone—a harder substance—formed a protective "cap" over the siltstone. This process created an umbrella-shaped rock that looks like a mushroom.

MAJOR CITIES

Omaha, with a population of 390,007, is the largest city in Nebraska. Located in eastern Nebraska near the Iowa border, it is home to the Henry Doorly Zoo. The 104-acre zoo boasts many unique exhibits, including an open-air **aviary** and a 70-foot underwater glass tunnel, where visitors can stand nose to nose with sharks and manta rays. The Joslyn Art Museum in Omaha features one of the largest collections of Western paintings in the United States.

Lincoln, the **capital** of Nebraska, is the second-largest city, with a population of 225,581. It is located in southeast Nebraska. Nebraska's **capitol,** which features a 400-foot-tall tower, took ten years to build. The building was designed by New York architect Bertram Grosvenor Goodhue, who won a 1920 national competition to design the capitol. Lincoln is also home to the University of Nebraska State Museum, which has the largest **fossil** collection in the United States and features the largest **mammoth** fossil ever found in the world (fifteen feet, seven inches tall).

Founded in the 1850s, Grand Island, population 42,940, is located in central Nebraska. It is home to the Stuhr Museum of the Prairie Pioneer, one of the top ten **living history museums** in the nation. At the Stuhr Museum, actors portray townspeople running businesses, attending church, and living the daily life of a settler in the 1800s.

Nebraska's Geography and Climate

Nebraska's geography differs greatly from west to east, from rolling sand hills to rich farm soil to craggy rock formations. Its weather, too, can have wide variations. Winter can bring blinding snowstorms, while summer can result in extreme heat, tornadoes, and violent windstorms.

LAND

Nebraska has two major land regions: the Dissected Till Plains in the eastern half of the state and the Great Plains in the west.

The Dissected Till Plains cover the eastern one-fifth of the state and also extend into South Dakota, Iowa, Missouri, and Kansas. A rich soil called **till** was left behind by the **glaciers** that covered this region until about 18,000 years ago. Because it has a high concentration of minerals, this soil is especially good for raising corn, wheat, oats, and other crops.

More than 8,000 acres of corn are planted and harvested each year.

The Badlands stretch north from Nebraska through South Dakota and North Dakota.

The Great Plains region, which makes up the western part of Nebraska, includes three different areas: the Loess Plain, the Sand Hills, and the High Plains. The Loess Plain, located in central Nebraska south of the Platte River, contains **fertile** farmland. North of the Loess Plain and the Platte River are the Sand Hills, which are low ridges of fine sand containing plenty of native grass to feed cattle. The third area in northwestern Nebraska is called the High Plains. This area receives little rainfall, and farmers must **irrigate** to raise crops there. The Badlands, in that same region, is a small area of unique **eroded** rock formations. The rugged, pointed rock cliffs are fascinating to tourists, but are of little use to farmers because they have very little soil or grass.

CLIMATE

Because it is located near the center of the **continental** United States and far from any ocean, Nebraska has a **temperate** climate, with average temperatures of 76°F in the summer and 23°F in the winter.

Eastern Nebraska receives the most rainfall, with an average of 27 inches each year, while western Nebraska receives considerably less, 18 inches a year. In recent years, western Nebraska has regularly experienced drought—or a severe shortage of rainfall. There has been up to nine inches less than the normal annual rainfall, which has caused rivers to dry up and crops to die in the fields.

July 24, 2000

Most Nebraskans have experienced severe thunderstorms or tornadoes, but on July 24, 2000, a supercell—or long-lasting severe thunderstorm—in South Dakota split in two, sending the right half of the storm into north-central Nebraska. For the next ten hours, the supercell spawned three confirmed tornadoes, all in rural areas, and dropped hailstones larger than two inches in diameter.

Nebraska experiences a period of severe thunderstorms almost every summer. Warm, moist breezes blowing north from the Gulf of Mexico, and cold, dry air blowing south from Canada can meet in Nebraska, causing unstable air patterns. The warm air tries to rise and the cold air blocks it. This causes an upward rotation of warm air that can produce highly dangerous thunderstorms that can result in tornadoes. Nebraska averages 39 tornadoes a year, the fifth highest of any state in the United States. Most of these tornadoes occur in May, June, or July.

There is a distinct difference in precipitation across the state. The west is dry, while the east receives a moderate amount of rain and snow.

Average Annual Precipitation Nebraska

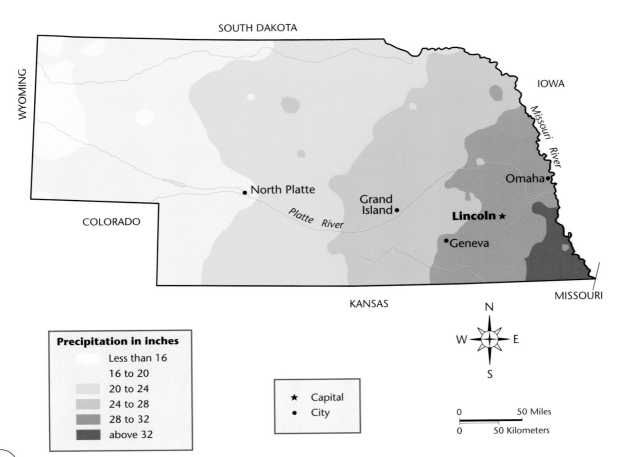

Famous Firsts

NATURE FIRSTS

In 1872 Nebraska citizens planted one million trees on the first Arbor Day, a holiday that encourages people to plant trees in their communities. The word *arbor* means shady garden. The idea for the holiday came from J. Sterling Morton, who moved to the Nebraska Territory from Detroit in 1854. Morton and his wife were great nature lovers who planted trees, shrubs, and flowers around their home. Morton missed seeing the trees that were so abundant in the eastern United States, and he recognized that trees helped hold soil in place and provided building materials and shade. Arbor Day became a legal holiday in Nebraska in 1885, and other states began observing it as well.

Dr. Charles Bessey, a professor of **botany** at the University of Nebraska, began planting pine trees in 1902 as an experiment to see if trees could grow in Nebraska's sand hills. The result today is the 22,000-acre Nebraska National Forest, considered the largest hand-planted forest in the world.

The Henry Doorly Zoo in Omaha has the world's second-largest open-air **aviary.** Built in 1983, it is a four-acre space with an elevated walkway where people can observe 500 different species of birds, including flamingos, storks, swans, and cranes.

J. Sterling Morton was one of America's first conservationists.

The Nebraska National Forest system includes three different forest areas and more than one million acres.

TECHNOLOGY FIRSTS

Dr. Frank Brewster recognized that technology would help him practice medicine. One day in 1919, he and a pilot traveled by airplane from Beaver City, Nebraska, to Herndon, Kansas, where Dr. Brewster performed emergency surgery to remove a piece of steel from an oil field-worker's skull. Dr. Brewster purchased his own airplane after he became impatient trying to reach patients by car on muddy and rough roads. He became known as the Flying Doctor, as he was the first doctor in the nation to use an airplane to reach patients. Very few individuals owned airplanes in 1919, and none were used for business. Dr. Brewster started a trend—two years later airplanes began to be used to deliver mail over long distances.

In 1926 Harold Edgerton, born in Fremont in 1903, was a college student at the Massachusetts Institute of Technology when he noted that by adjusting the flashes of a **stroboscope** he could see parts of a running engine as if they were standing still. He applied this technology to cameras, "freezing" objects in motion so they could be

Photos such as this are known as "Edgerton photos" after their inventor.

captured on film. His photos featured fast-moving objects that cannot be seen by the human eye, such as a bullet piercing an apple or a hummingbird's flapping wings. These unique photos were featured in *LIFE* and *National Geographic.* In 1937 Edgerton invented the first underwater camera, which was used to photograph the *Titanic* after its discovery in the Atlantic Ocean in 1986.

In 1983 doctors at the University of Nebraska Medical Center in Omaha performed the first **bone marrow** transplant in the United States. People who have leukemia or similar serious illnesses have diseased blood cells. In a bone marrow transplant, the diseased cells are removed from the body and replaced with healthy cells. These healthy cells can come from a donor, or someone who shares his or her cells with the patient. Once a patient receives the healthy cells, he or she can sometimes recover from a serious illness more quickly than just by taking medication.

As a child, Edwin Perkins experimented with things in the kitchen of his family's home.

OTHER FIRSTS

Buffalo Bill Cody, a famous **scout** and hunter from the 1800s, organized the first rodeo, which is a competition for cowboys and cowgirls to show their skills at buffalo riding, calf roping, and horse racing. The first rodeo in the United States, called the "Old Glory Blowout," was held in North Platte on July 4, 1882. This rodeo is still held today in North Platte, during Nebraskaland Days each year in June.

Mail-order salesman Edwin Perkins of Hastings was fascinated by chemistry and enjoyed inventing things. In 1927, inspired by the success of Jell-O gelatin, Perkins removed the liquid from one of his popular products, a concentrated fruit drink called Fruit Smack. This left a powder that could be mixed with water. Perkins called his new product Kool-Aid. The flavors available then were strawberry, cherry, orange, lemon-lime, grape, and raspberry. Many flavors were developed over the years.

The system of using a single phone number, 911, to call police, medical professionals, or firefighters in an emergency was developed and first used in Lincoln in the late 1960s. This is the emergency calling system still in use today throughout the United States.

Nebraska's State Symbols

NEBRASKA STATE FLAG

Nebraska adopted a "state banner" in 1925. In 1963 the legislature voted to make this banner the official state flag. The blue background of the flag is the "national blue" color in the U.S. flag.

NEBRASKA STATE SEAL

The state seal was adopted in 1867. It features a smith, or metal worker, using a hammer and anvil, which symbolizes industry, and a cabin surrounded by fields of wheat and corn, which symbolizes the state's early farmers. The seal also has a steamboat traveling the Missouri River and a train heading toward the Rocky Mountains. They were forms of transportation that helped new settlers come to Nebraska.

Nebraska was one of the last states in the U.S. to adopt a state flag. They adopted the flag nearly 100 years after becoming a state.

In contrast to the flag, the Great Seal of the State of Nebraska was adopted only months after achieving statehood.

State Motto: "Equality Before the Law"

When the state motto, "Equality Before the Law," was adopted in 1867 as part of the state seal, it referred to every settler's right to claim land in the state. According to the **Homestead Act** passed by the U.S. Congress in 1862, every free man who was at least 21 years old could claim 160 acres of government land. During this time, settlers claimed about 30 percent of the land in Nebraska. The state motto also speaks to the **abolition** of **slavery** in 1866 and the right of African Americans to become homesteaders. No longer slaves, they were "equal before the law," with the same rights as any other settler.

"Beautiful Nebraska"

Beautiful Nebraska, peaceful prairieland,

Laced with many rivers, and the hills of sand;

Dark green valleys cradled in the earth,

Rain and sunshine bring abundant birth.

Beautiful Nebraska, as you look around,

You will find a rainbow reaching to the ground;

All these wonders by the Master's hand;

Beautiful Nebraska land.

We are so proud of this state where we live,

There is no place that has so much to give.

Beautiful Nebraska, as you look around,

You will find a rainbow reaching to the ground;

All these wonders by the Master's hand;

Beautiful Nebraska land.

State Song: "Beautiful Nebraska"

In 1960 Jim Fras composed the song "Beautiful Nebraska." He tells the story of lying in a pasture and observing the land around him, which led to the words of the song: "Beautiful Nebraska, peaceful prairieland. Laced with many rivers and the hills of sand." In 1967 the Nebraska legislature declared "Beautiful Nebraska" to be the state song.

State Nickname: The Cornhusker State

In 1945 the Nebraska legislature changed the official state nickname from the Tree Planters State to the Cornhusker State. One of Ne-

Goldenrod grows from July to October each year throughout the state.

braska's leading crops is corn, and someone who removes the husk—the dry outer layer covering an ear of corn—by hand is called a cornhusker. Before there were machines to remove the husks from ears of corn, people had to do it with their hands, and many small towns held cornhusking competitions for fun.

STATE FLOWER: GOLDENROD

Goldenrod, a two-foot-tall herb with small yellow flowers, was declared the state flower by Nebraska's legislature in 1895. Numerous species of this **perennial** plant grow throughout Nebraska.

STATE TREE: COTTONWOOD

The American elm was Nebraska's first official state tree, but in 1972 the legislature changed it to the cottonwood because of its association with pioneer Nebraska. Early settlers were fond of this tall tree with full, broad leaves that grows throughout the state. They frequently collected cottonwood shoots, or young trees, and planted them on their homesteads. The cottonwood tree is known for its seeds, carried on cottonlike tufts that float in the wind.

The western meadowlark feeds mainly on insects and seeds.

STATE BIRD: WESTERN MEADOWLARK

The western meadowlark has a bright yellow breast and a cheery song. Because it is common throughout the state, legislators designated it the state bird in 1929. The western meadowlark builds its nests in grassy fields, or meadows.

A female white-tailed deer, such as this one, can weigh up to 200 pounds.

STATE MAMMAL: WHITE-TAILED DEER

The white-tailed deer, a plant-eating mammal commonly found in farmlands and wooded areas, was declared the state mammal in 1981. When in danger, this deer raises its tail to display a bright patch of white hair, a signal to other deer or **fawns** to run away quickly.

STATE GRASS: LITTLE BLUESTEM GRASS

Little bluestem grass was named the state grass in 1969. It grows throughout the Great Plains of Nebraska, often in large clumps. It is sometimes referred to as "bunch grass." It is **native** to Nebraska and survives in sandy regions where little else will grow, making it an important source of food for cattle.

The largest channel catfish ever caught in Nebraska was 41 pounds, 8 ounces.

STATE FISH: CHANNEL CATFISH

Nebraskans love to catch and eat channel catfish, declared the state fish in 1997. These fish lay their eggs in "channels," or underwater cavities created among tree roots and rocks in the rivers running throughout the state.

STATE INSECT: HONEYBEE

Honey production is a $3 million industry in Nebraska. Thus, the state legislature named the honey-

Honeybees help to pollinate plants such as clover, cotton, and sunflowers.

bee the state insect in 1975. There are approximately 60,000 honeybee colonies in the state that produce more than 4 million pounds of honey.

STATE FOSSIL: MAMMOTH

Fossils from the **mammoth,** a prehistoric elephant-like mammal that lived in North America, have been found in every county in Nebraska. The mammoth was named the state fossil in 1967 and one of the largest mammoth fossils in the world—fifteen feet, seven inches tall—was discovered in Lincoln County. It is now displayed at the University of Nebraska State Museum in Lincoln.

The Lincoln County mammoth weighed more than fifteen tons, or 30,000 pounds.

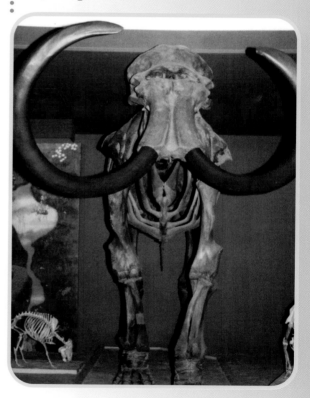

STATE GEMSTONE: BLUE AGATE

Blue agate, or blue chalcedony, is commonly found in northwest Nebraska and was named the state gemstone in 1967. This stone is smooth and pale with blue and white stripes.

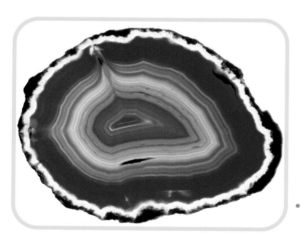

Blue agate is often used in jewelry.

Nebraska's History and People

Explorers in the early 1800s described the Nebraska Territory as a land of prairie grasses and sandy hills, occupied by Native Americans who hunted buffalo and raised crops for their food. With the passage of the **Homestead Act** in 1862 and its offer of free land, Nebraska became attractive to many thousands of new settlers.

The roots of prairie grass grow so deep and close together that Nebraska's early settlers found the soil hard to plow for farming.

EARLY PEOPLES

There is archaeological evidence that people lived in western Nebraska as long ago as 8000 B.C.E., although there is little known about any of Nebraska's early settlers until the 1600s, when Native Americans established villages there. Throughout the 1700s Native Americans were the sole inhabitants of Nebraska. The Omaha, Ponca, and Oto tribes lived near the Missouri River in the east, the Pawnee tribe inhabited central Nebraska, and the Sioux and Cheyenne tribes lived in northern Nebraska.

EARLY EXPLORERS

In 1803 President Thomas Jefferson paid $15 million to France for the Louisiana Territory. The Louisiana Terri-

tory, which included the area that would become Nebraska, doubled the size of the United States. The same year, President Thomas Jefferson sent an **expedition** led by U.S. Army officers Meriwether Lewis and William Clark to explore this new territory. By 1804 Lewis and Clark reached what is today Nebraska and met with the Oto and Missouri tribes at Council Bluff, north of present-day Omaha. Although the Native Americans had seen French and Spanish explorers in the area, Lewis and Clark were the first American explorers to meet with the Oto and Missouri tribes.

Fort Atkinson was built on the site of Lewis and Clark's historic meeting with the Oto and Missouri tribes at Council Bluff.

Fur-trading expeditions sent some of the first wagons through Nebraska in the 1830s on what would become known as the Oregon Trail. By the 1840s hundreds of thousands of travelers were making their way—by wagon, on horseback, or on foot—along the trail across Nebraska to establish homesteads in Oregon and California. The Oregon Trail followed the Little Blue River, crossed a stretch of dry land to the Platte River, and then followed the Platte River into Wyoming. It is estimated that, in a 30-year period, 350,000

Great American Desert

On an 1820 expedition across Nebraska, U.S. Army major Stephen H. Long and his group of twenty men followed the Platte River Valley west to the Rocky Mountains. After observing the sandy hills and dry plains of Nebraska, a member of Long's group wrote that the region could never be farmed. At the top of their map of this region, they wrote in bold letters the words "Great American Desert." Their recommendation was that the land should be left to the hunters and bison and other animals, and that settlers would never be interested in living there. More than a century later, in the 1930s, **irrigation** made it possible for farmers to use every inch of the dry land for farming.

people traveled through Nebraska on the Oregon Trail on their way to other places. The passage of the Homestead Act in 1862 prompted some of those travelers to settle in Nebraska.

THE KANSAS–NEBRASKA ACT

The U.S. Congress passed the Kansas–Nebraska Act in 1854, creating the territories of Kansas and Nebraska. When California became a state in 1850, members of the U.S. Congress began debating over where to build a railroad that would cross the continent. Senator Stephen Douglas of Illinois wanted a route that led west from Chicago, Illinois, through the Platte River Valley in Nebraska, to San Francisco, California. Before such a railroad could be built, the area around it needed an organized government to protect it against attacks by Native Americans and Congress needed to vote on whether building it would legalize **slavery.** The Kansas–Nebraska Act repealed the language of the 1820 **Missouri Compromise,** which legalized slavery only in southern states. Unlike the states in the south, the newly established governments in the Kansas and Nebraska territories could decide for themselves whether they would legalize slavery. While the Nebraska legislature never voted to make slavery legal, there were slaves in Nebraska who had been brought by settlers from southern states. The legislature later took formal action on the matter, voting to make Nebraska a free territory.

SETTLING THE GREAT PLAINS

In the mid-1850s Native Americans lived throughout the territory of Nebraska. Settlers could buy or obtain land from the U.S. government at $1.25 per acre at auctions or by being a squatter. A squatter was a person who moved onto public land before it was surveyed, or measured and recorded by the government. When Congress passed the

Homestead Act of 1862, any settler who was at least 21 years old and who had not fought against the United States during the **Civil War** (1861–1865) could claim 160 acres of land. After living there five years, the homesteader had to prove he or she had improved the land by building a home or raising crops. This allowed the homesteader to become the legal owner. Thousands of settlers came to Nebraska to claim their land under the Homestead Act. For the first time in Nebraska's history, people were staying in the territory instead of passing through to settle in other areas.

Thousands of covered wagons, like these, moved across the Great Plains as settlers looked to find new land to call home.

STATEHOOD

In 1867 the Nebraska Territory became the 37th state. However, the journey to statehood had a few challenges. The U.S. Congress debated in 1864 and again in 1866 about Nebraska's statehood. A statement in the proposed Nebraska state constitution said African Americans—who were slaves in other states but not in the Nebraska Territory—were not allowed to vote. Congress took those words out of the **bill,** causing President Andrew Johnson to **veto** the bill. Congress passed the bill in spite of the president's veto. On March 1, 1867, President Johnson reluctantly signed the proclamation that made Nebraska a state.

NATIVE AMERICAN WARS

As settlers claimed land and built homes in Nebraska in the 1800s, the U.S. government ordered Native Americans to relocate to **reservations.** Settlers traveling through Nebraska to western mining towns or mail carriers on

Living in Sod Houses

Because there were few trees in the plains region of Nebraska, settlers in the late 1800s made their homes from sod, or dirt packed tightly with grass roots. Sod was sliced from the ground in three-foot-long pieces and stacked to make walls. Sod homes—or "soddies," as they were sometimes called—were small and dark, leaky when it rained, and sometimes infested with bugs. As trains brought lumber from East Coast cities to Nebraska, settlers built new homes of wood and used their old sod houses as storage sheds or barns.

horseback often passed through Native American hunting grounds. The tribes, feeling threatened by these disruptions, began a series of attacks on settlers in the 1850s. The U.S. Army built forts in Nebraska and other territories and sent its soldiers to help keep peace as settlers tried to gain more land. At Fort Robinson, for example, the government distributed food, clothing, tools, and supplies to Native Americans in exchange for land. Despite many battles to preserve their land, by 1877 most Native Americans were forced to live on reservations.

Red Cloud was one of the most important Lakota leaders of the 1800s.

FAMOUS PEOPLE

Red Cloud (1822–1909), Native American **advocate** and Lakota tribal leader. Born near the forks of the Platte River, Red Cloud spent his early years in battle with other Native American tribes. He became well-known for his ability to plan successful battles. His assaults on U.S. forts along the Bozeman Trail in Wyoming—the heart of Lakota territory—resulted in the Fort Laramie Treaty of 1868 and the government's agreement to abandon those forts. In 1877, even after the defeat of his tribe, Red Cloud continued to serve as a spokesperson for the preservation of Native American identity.

William Jennings Bryan was known as "the Great Commoner" because his public speaking appealed to so many people.

William Jennings Bryan (1860–1925), politician and speaker. Bryan attended law school in Illinois, then moved to Nebraska, and, in 1890, became the second **Democrat** to be elected to the state legislature. He won the Democratic nomination for president of the United States three times, but lost the elections to William McKinley and William H. Taft. Using his skills as an orator, or public speaker, he used words as a weapon against policies he considered unfair to ordinary citizens who did not have money and power.

Grace Abbott (1878–1939), social worker and professor. During the **Great Depression** of the 1930s, Abbott, who was from Grand Island, was the most powerful woman in the government as head of the U.S. Children's Bureau. She campaigned to end child labor and helped plan the Social Security Act, which provided financial assistance to individuals in need.

Grover Cleveland Alexander (1887–1950), baseball pitcher. A St. Paul native, Alexander played for the Philadelphia Phillies, Chicago Cubs, and St. Louis Cardinals. A Hall of Fame honoree, he overcame **epilepsy** and injuries he received while serving in **World War I** to become one of the greatest pitchers in baseball history. No other National League pitcher has ever beat Grover Cleveland Alexander's record of 373 victories and 90 shutouts.

Jay W. Forrester (1918–   ), inventor. As a child, Forrester—from Climax—built a wind-driven electrical system using car parts to give his home electricity. In 1949, while working for the U.S. military, Forrester designed magnetic core memory, a way for computers to store data that became the standard in the computer industry.

Marlon Brando (1924–   ), actor. Brando, born in Omaha, studied acting in New York City and performed

The Autobiography of Malcolm X has become a widely read book since his death in 1965.

on Broadway before getting his big-screen break in the 1947 film *A Streetcar Named Desire.* He has starred in 43 movies, including *On the Waterfront, Guys and Dolls,* and *Superman.*

Malcolm X (1925–1965), civil rights advocate. Born Malcolm Little in Omaha, Malcolm X watched his father—a Baptist preacher and advocate for the right of African Americans to have equal job and social opportunity—die a violent death. Malcolm X later became a follower of the Nation of Islam, a Muslim organization that taught that white society kept African Americans from reaching their potential. One of the Nation of Islam's goals was for African Americans to have a state separate from white society, and Malcolm X traveled throughout the United States speaking about these beliefs. He was killed during a speaking engagement in New York City in 1965.

Johnny Carson's television show led the way for later TV shows featuring Jay Leno and David Letterman.

Johnny Carson (1925–), television host. Carson spent most of his childhood in Norfolk, Nebraska, where he began his career at age fourteen with a magic act he called "The Great Carsoni." While in the navy during **World War II,** he entertained his fellow soldiers with humorous stories and later worked at a Nebraska radio station writing comedy bits and commercials. Carson headed to Hollywood in 1950, where he worked as a writer for comedian Red Skelton's television program. Skelton suffered a concussion from an on-set accident right before airtime one evening, and Carson filled in at the last minute, receiving rave reviews for his performance. He was featured on several daytime shows before landing a spot on *The Tonight Show,* which he hosted for 30 years. Carson won six **Emmy awards** for his work.

Father Flanagan's Girls and Boys Town

Girls and Boys Town, a village west of Omaha with its own zip code, is a place where neglected and abandoned children have gone to live for the past 85 years.

FOUNDING BOYS TOWN

In 1917, Father Edward J. Flanagan, an Irish Catholic priest, saw many young boys wandering the streets of Omaha who needed a place to live and an adult to care about them. He found a large house in Omaha and asked a friend to help him pay the $90 monthly rent so he could offer a home to these boys. Over the next few months, the number of boys living in the home grew from 12 to 50, and Father Flanagan found

The "Two Brothers" statue features the famous saying, "He ain't heavy, Father . . . he's m' brother."

he needed a much larger house. He located 160 acres of land west of Omaha with a house, barns, chicken coops, and a garage. It was not for sale, but the owner listened to Father Flanagan's story and agreed to let him have the property with the expectation that he raise and sell some crops to pay for it. Father Flanagan, a crew of his boys, and some volunteer citizens from Omaha added a school and a chapel to the land. Boys Town was founded on October 22, 1921.

LIFE IN BOYS TOWN

Father Flanagan believed a good education was very important, so the boys attended a regular school on the campus of Boys Town. In the summer, they learned how to farm, growing vegetables and raising chickens to sell to help support Boys Town. Some Omaha citizens thought of Boys Town as a prison for children who had broken the law, but Father Flanagan considered the boys to be one large family. He created a homelike atmosphere, refusing to put fences around Boys Town and gathering the group daily for meals and chapel time.

Girls and Boys Town continues to provide help to more than 1,800 children each year.

Boys Town grew quickly. By 1936, when it became an official municipality—or city—of the state of Nebraska, it had 200 residents.

BOYS TOWN TODAY

Father Flanagan died in 1948, but his work was continued by other Catholic priests, who helped Boys Town grow to 900 acres near Omaha and 19 other sites in 14 states. In 1979 the leaders of Boys Town changed the name to Girls and Boys Town and began accepting girls to their program, too. The original Boys Town location now covers 900 acres of land, including 400 acres of farms and 95 buildings (60 buildings for residences and 35 buildings for school, recreation, and church). In the 1970s and 1980s, Girls and Boys Town expanded its program to help children with speech, hearing, and learning problems. Today it also offers classes to help children learn to read and to teach parenting skills to adults.

Boys Town: The Movie

This 1938 movie, which starred Spencer Tracy and Mickey Rooney, brought Boys Town to the attention of the nation causing U.S. citizens to donate money to help fund the programs at Boys Town. It also prompted the U.S. government and other countries to ask Father Flanagan's advice on how to care for children who did not have their own families. In the 1940s Father Flanagan traveled to Japan, Asia, and Europe to tell the story of Boys Town.  These other countries soon established similar programs for young boys. The publicity surrounding the movie not only made Father Flanagan well-known beyond the borders of Nebraska. In addition, it resulted in hundreds of other children being helped worldwide through similar programs.

Nebraska's State Government

Nebraska's present constitution, or system of laws and principles making up its state government, was adopted in 1875. Like the federal government, Nebraska's government is made up of the legislative, executive, and judicial branches. The work of the government is done in Lincoln, the state capital.

LEGISLATIVE BRANCH

Nebraska has a unique form of state government. It is the only state with a unicameral, or one-house, legislature. The 49 members of its legislature are called senators. Voters elect these legislators on a **nonpartisan** ballot, meaning there are no political parties, such as Republicans or **Democrats,** listed on the ballot. Voters approved the nonpartisan unicameral legislature in 1934.

Each Nebraska senator serves a four-year term. The legislature meets for 60 days in even-numbered years and

Lincoln is home to Nebraska's state government and its largest university, the University of Nebraska.

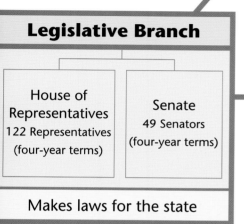

Executive Branch

Governor and Lt. Governor
(four-year terms)

Carries out the laws of the state

Legislative Branch

House of Representatives 122 Representatives (four-year terms)	Senate 49 Senators (four-year terms)

Makes laws for the state

Judicial Branch

Supreme Court
7 Justices (six-year terms)

Court of Appeals
10 Judges (eight-year terms)

Circuit Courts
55 Judges (four-year terms)

Explains laws

for 90 days in odd-numbered years. The legislative branch is responsible for creating the state's laws. A senator can introduce a new idea for a law as a **bill.** The legislature then votes to accept, **amend,** or reject the bill. If a bill is approved, it becomes a law.

EXECUTIVE BRANCH

The executive branch is made up of the governor, lieutenant governor, secretary of state, attorney general, treasurer, and auditor. These leaders are elected to a four-year term. The governor oversees all operations of the state government. The lieutenant governor is second in command. The attorney general ensures the state's laws are followed, and the treasurer and auditor make sure taxes are collected to provide the money the state needs to conduct its business, such as building roads and operating public schools.

The state capitol in Lincoln was built between 1922 and 1932.

JUDICIAL BRANCH

The judicial branch of Nebraska's government is made up of the state supreme court, the court of appeals, 12 district courts, and 59 county courts.

The supreme court has a chief justice and six judges. Its role is to provide leadership for the state's judicial system and to hear appeals, or court cases transferred for a new hearing, which sometimes go to the court of appeals first. Each judge is selected through a merit plan, created in 1964. Under this plan, the governor chooses a judge whenever there is a vacancy. After that judge has served for three years, voters can choose to keep him or her for another six-year term.

The district courts decide cases of felonies, or serious crimes such as murder, as well as lawsuits between individuals for amounts of money greater than $45,000. Juvenile courts in three counties hear cases related to minors, or children younger than eighteen years old. Some court cases are about children who are accused of committing a crime, while others are about children whose parents have not provided adequate care for them. The county courts decide cases of misdemeanors, or less serious crimes such as traffic violations. If someone were required to appear in court for a speeding ticket, he or she would go to a county court.

The supreme court not only oversees the court system but also all the lawyers as well.

Nebraska's Culture

Nebraska's annual festivals and cultural events recall the state's history and heritage.

NATIVE AMERICAN HERITAGE

There are about 12,500 Native Americans living in Nebraska today, from the Winnebago, Omaha, Ponca, and Santee Sioux tribes. These Native Americans hold annual powwows, or celebrations.

The Omaha Powwow, a harvest celebration held for three days each August at the Omaha Reservation in Macy, features tribal music, dancing, and authentic Native American food such as hot fry bread. The clothing worn by tribal members at the powwow is made from buckskin, beads, and bird feathers, natural materials originally used by Native Americans in the 1700s and 1800s. This powwow, held since 1805, is considered the longest running harvest celebration in the state.

The five-day Winnebago Powwow, held in Winnebago each July, offers ceremonial songs and competitions among Native American dancers. Intertribal dancing also is featured.

The Omaha Powwow is held during the weekend of the first full moon each August.

The Buffalo Bill Rodeo is modeled after Buffalo Bill's Wild West show, which toured the country in the late 1800's.

THE HERITAGE OF THE OLD WEST

Nebraska's Old West heritage is evident in its rodeos and reenactments of cowboy culture. Nebraska's Big Rodeo at Burwell, held each July since 1931, offers horse shows as well as calf-roping and steer-riding competitions.

Nebraskaland Days in North Platte, declared the official state celebration by the 1965 legislature, lasts for almost two weeks each June. It offers the Buffalo Bill Rodeo, with its calf-roping and bareback horse-riding competitions. Nebraskaland Days also features concerts by country musicians, a parade, and breakfast served out of a chuck wagon, or a wagon with food and cooking utensils like those used by settlers in the 1800s.

More than 300,000 people visit the Nebraska State Fair each year.

The Nebraska State Fair, held each year in Lincoln from late August to early September, features exhibits of items made by Nebraskans, farm machinery, and livestock. In recent years, the fair has added such events as a sampling of wines made from Nebraska grapes; a display of works by regional artists; and "Nebraska's Largest Classroom," a one-day field trip to the fair for elementary students.

Nebraska's Food

Nebraska's food has been influenced by **immigrants** from European countries such as Germany, Poland, and Denmark. Recipes for foods such as bierocks—a baked bun stuffed with cabbage, meat, and onions—have a German-Russian influence. Descendants of Polish families share a love of sausage dishes. At Grundlovs Fest, a festival held each June in Dannebrog—the self-proclaimed Danish capital of Nebraska—visitors can sample meatball dishes and pastries.

Nebraska is the top state in the meat processing industry, with 21 percent of the nation's commercial cattle slaughter. One of its most famous beef suppliers, Omaha

Beef hangs in abattoirs, or slaughter houses, before it is processed into steaks or hamburgers.

33

Golden Corn Bread

Here is a recipe made with cornmeal, a product of Nebraska's leading crop.

Have an adult help you.

1 cup sifted flour	$\frac{1}{2}$ teaspoon salt
1 cup yellow cornmeal	1 egg
3 teaspoons baking powder	1 cup milk
	$\frac{1}{4}$ cup soft shortening
$\frac{1}{4}$ cup sugar	

Sift flour once, measure, add cornmeal, baking powder, sugar, and salt and sift into a medium bowl. Add egg, milk, and shortening and beat with a spoon for about one minute. Bake in a greased eight-inch square pan in a 425°F oven for about twenty minutes.

Steaks, was founded in 1917 and ships filet mignon and other cuts of beef all over the world. Nebraskans love steak, whether it is grilled, cubed on a skewer for kabobs, or breaded for country-fried steak.

Nebraska's Folklore and Legends

Nebraska's legends and folklore—or stories passed down from one generation to the next—are filled with images of hearty **pioneers** who loved the land. Folklore is a mix of truth and fiction. The stories help teach lessons in an easily understandable, entertaining way.

DROUGHT BUSTER

Farmers rely on rain to help their crops grow, and a drought—or period of no rainfall—can cause them much concern. In this folktale from the 1800s, a Swedish immigrant named Febold Feboldson became frustrated with the drought not because he was a farmer but because the ponds had dried up. He could no longer go fishing. He built bonfires around all of the lakes in the area, hoping to create enough heat to cause the water in the lakes to evaporate and form rain clouds. According to legend,

Feboldson added logs to the bonfires day and night and eventually his plan worked. Clouds formed with water from the lakes, and rain fell on the dry plains. His neighbors, although happy to see rain, complained to him that the lakes had dried up and there was no place to swim!

NATIVE AMERICAN LEGENDS

A Lakota legend tells of a woman who gathered corn from the field to store for the winter. After she had gathered all the corn she could see, she turned to go home and a child's voice called to her: "No, don't leave me! Don't go away without me!" She searched the field for a long time, finally locating a small ear of corn under some leaves. She believed the corn spoke to her as a reminder that the crop should always be carefully gathered, so as not to waste even the smallest ear of corn.

A Cheyenne story tells of a tribe that could not feed its members. A young man named Little Brave volunteered to explore a mysterious cave near the tribe's camp to search for food. He met an elderly woman in the cave who showed him a vision of buffalo and gave him three pans of meat to share with his tribe. When members of the tribe awoke the next morning, hundreds of buffalo surrounded them on the plains. They believed the Sky Spirits had shown them mercy and provided for their needs.

Buffalo have been used for their hide and for food throughout history.

Nebraska's Sports Teams

Because Nebraska does not have any major professional sports teams, Nebraskans are fiercely loyal fans of their college teams.

UNIVERSITY OF NEBRASKA CORNHUSKERS

Each time the University of Nebraska Cornhuskers football team plays at Memorial Stadium in Lincoln, a sea of football fans wearing red, the school color, enthusiastically greets them. In fact, there have been an average of 75,000 fans in attendance at every home game for the past 30 years. The team has won five National Collegiate Athletic Association (NCAA) national football championships since 1971, and the Cornhuskers also have many players in the National Football League, including Green Bay Packers running back Ahman Green.

Football is not the only well-known sport at the University of Nebraska. Fifty-six members of the university's women's swim team have earned All-American honors

In 1995 Nebraska won one of the most lopsided championship games in NCAA football history. That year, they beat the Florida Gators, 62–24.

Penny Heyns broke 14 world records during her swimming career.

since 1988. The most famous team member, Penny Heyns, won two gold medals in the breaststroke competition at the 1996 Olympic games in Atlanta, Georgia.

CREIGHTON UNIVERSITY

Creighton University, in Omaha, is the home of the Bluejays. St. Louis Cardinals player and Major League Hall of Fame member Bob Gibson got his start in baseball at Creighton in the 1950s. Creighton University hosts the NCAA Men's College World Series baseball competition each year at Johnny Rosenblatt Stadium.

Creighton University pitcher Tom Oldham faces the University of Notre Dame at Rosenblatt Stadium.

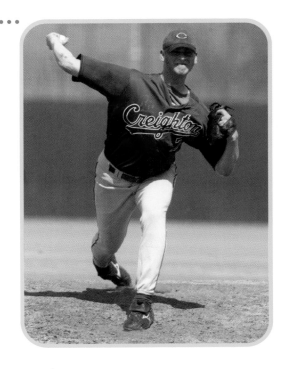

Nebraska's Businesses and Products

Nebraska's diverse economy includes agriculture, food-processing businesses, banking, and health care.

AGRICULTURE

One of every four jobs in Nebraska is tied to agriculture, the business of raising animals and crops used to make food. The 55,000 farms and ranches in Nebraska take up 96 percent of the state's land. The average farmer owns 859 acres of land and raises cattle, corn, soybeans, or hogs. The largest farms are cattle ranches in the central part of the state, some of which cover up to 100,000 acres. Smaller farms in eastern Nebraska raise wheat and oats in addition to the crops mentioned above.

Livestock, or animals raised to be sold for profit, provides 60 percent of Nebraska's annual $3.5 billion agriculture income. Nebraska's Cherry County has 170,000 cows, the most cows in one county in the nation.

Nebraska ranks first in the nation in commercial cattle slaughter. It handles 16 percent of the nation's commercial cattle production. Ranchers in central Nebraska ship calves to eastern Nebraska, where they feed on corn and grow fat before they are sold to beef producers.

Hogs are the second most important livestock product in the state, and Nebraska is sixth in the nation for commercial hog production. There are 1.8 million hogs in

Livestock, especially cattle, are at the center of Nebraska's economy.

Nebraska, adding $243 million to the state's agriculture revenue.

Crops provide one-third of Nebraska's $3.5 billion annual agriculture income. Corn is the state's leading crop and is grown mostly in eastern Nebraska. About 40 percent of this corn is used to feed livestock. Nebraska ranks first in the nation in soybean production and third in corn production. Other leading crops include milo and wheat, grains used in food production.

Aquifers and Farming

The state of Nebraska hides huge quantities of water. The Ogallala **Aquifer,** an underground water-bearing rock formation, is the largest aquifer in the United States. It is the size of California, and it reaches from South Dakota to Texas, with two-thirds of the water located under Nebraska. This aquifer makes it possible for farmers to irrigate about eight million acres of cropland that get very little rainfall each year. Nebraskans also rely on the aquifer as a source of drinking water for their cities.

FOOD PROCESSING

There are more than 300 businesses in Nebraska dedicated to food processing, or the preparation, packaging, marketing, and transporting of meats and other foods. In the 1970s meat-processing plants were relocated from Omaha and Chicago to smaller cities in Nebraska such as Grand Island, Dakota City, West Point, and Madison. By creating more plants closer together, animals could be transported by truck instead of by railroad.

ConAgra, a major distributor of food products, was established in 1919 in Omaha. ConAgra processes and packages meat, and produces seasonings and grain products. Its consumer brands are well-known: Hunt's, Armour, Parkay, Butterball, and Chef Boyardee, among others.

SERVICE INDUSTRIES

Businesses providing services to customers—including banks, health-care providers, engineering firms, and repair shops—bring the most annual revenue to Nebraska. Mutual of Omaha, one of the largest insurance companies in the United States, is the fourth-largest employer in Nebraska. It was established in 1909 and has always been headquartered in Omaha.

OFFUTT AIR FORCE BASE

Offutt Air Force Base, Omaha's top employer with about 10,000 employees, is the headquarters for the U.S. Strategic Command, which is responsible for the planning and wartime operations of the U.S. nuclear forces. It is also home to the Air Force Weather Agency, a 24-hour center providing forecasts to the U.S. president, the Department of Defense, and U.S. Army and Air Force fighter planes.

Situated on approximately 2,000 acres of land, Offutt Air Force Base is one of the largest military bases in the United States.

Attractions and Landmarks

Visitors to Nebraska can enjoy a variety of historic and outdoor attractions, many of which are closely tied to Nebraska's unique history.

HISTORIC ATTRACTIONS

At 22,000 acres, Fort Robinson State Park near Chadron is Nebraska's largest state park. Fort Robinson was an active military post from 1874 to 1948 and the site of Chief Crazy Horse's death during a battle with the military in 1877. Visitors can tour the park by train or stagecoach to see the canyons and buffalo herds or stop at campgrounds, theaters, and restaurants. Exhibits are housed in the original 1905 post headquarters. Some exhibits include military items from the fort and the Sioux Ghost Dance shirt, which was believed to make the Sioux invisible.

The Buffalo Bill Scouts Rest Ranch State Historical Park in North Platte sits on 25 acres of the original homestead

Fort Robinson State Park features dozens of hiking and horse-riding trails.

established by William F. "Buffalo Bill" Cody, famous buffalo hunter and scout. Visitors can tour his home and the original barn, where films from Cody's Wild West show, which toured the United States and Europe in the late 1800s and early 1900s, are shown. Horseback rides are available on the adjacent 233-acre recreation area.

The Willa Cather House in Red Cloud, the author's childhood home, is surrounded by five other restored historic buildings, including a church and bank, all featured in Cather's novels. Nearby, the 609-acre Willa Cather Memorial Prairie once inspired Cather to write, "that shaggy grass country had gripped me with a passion that I never have been able to shake."

The Pioneer Experience

Author Willa Cather moved with her family from Virginia to Red Cloud, Nebraska, in 1884 when she was nine years old. Though she lived in Red Cloud for only the next six years, her experiences while living among pioneers shaped her many novels. These novels include *O Pioneers!*, *My Antonia*, and *One of Ours*, for which she won a **Pulitzer Prize** in 1922. Cather paints pictures of the harshness of pioneer life and also of the hope that filled the immigrant settlers who came to Nebraska seeking opportunities for land ownership, homes, and jobs.

OUTDOOR ATTRACTIONS

Archaeological **excavations** in the area now known as Ash Hollow State Historical Park, near Lewellen, have indicated that humans lived there as long as 6,000 years ago. The fossil remains of a prehistoric rhinoceros, **mammoths,** and mastodons, which are elephant-like mammals, have all been discovered there. Visitors can hike nature trails in the park and see a cave where prehistoric people lived. The visitor center is situated on a bluff offering a view that spans for miles.

Places to see in Nebraska

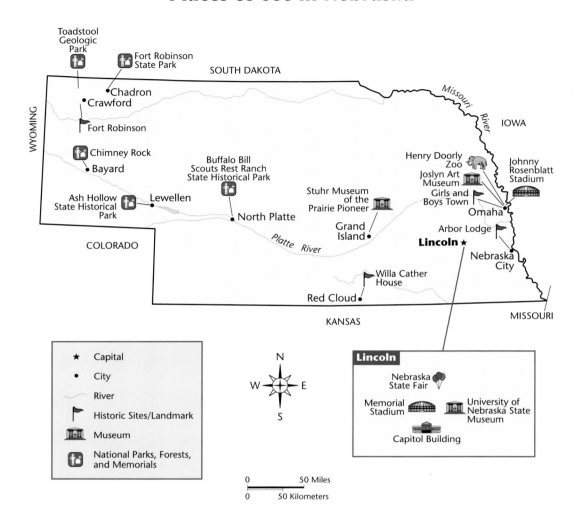

Toadstool Geologic Park

Fort Robinson State Park

SOUTH DAKOTA

•Chadron
• Crawford

WYOMING

Fort Robinson

Chimney Rock
• Bayard

Buffalo Bill
Scouts Rest Ranch
State Historical Park

Ash Hollow
State Historical
Park

• Lewellen

• North Platte

Stuhr Museum
of the
Prairie Pioneer

Platte River

Grand
Island •

COLORADO

Missouri River

IOWA

Henry Doorly
Zoo

Joslyn Art
Museum

Girls and
Boys Town

Omaha

Johnny
Rosenblatt
Stadium

Arbor Lodge

Lincoln ★

Nebraska
City

Willa Cather
House

Red Cloud •

KANSAS

MISSOURI

Legend

- ★ Capital
- • City
- ～ River
- ⚑ Historic Sites/Landmark
- 🏛 Museum
- National Parks, Forests, and Memorials

N
W ✦ E
S

Lincoln

Nebraska
State Fair

Memorial
Stadium

University of
Nebraska State
Museum

Capitol Building

0   50 Miles
0   50 Kilometers

Erosion created Chimney Rock and, unfortunately, erosion will destroy it one day.

Chimney Rock is a 325-foot-tall rock spire rising up from the prairie near Bayard. Its shape has been compared to an upside-down funnel or a child's sand castle, and is made of clay and sandstone. Chimney Rock could be seen for miles by travelers along the Oregon Trail in the 1800s. It was mentioned in the journals and diaries of those travelers more often than any other natural formation along the trail. A visitor center features original sketches of Chimney Rock and maps made by early explorers.

Map of Nebraska

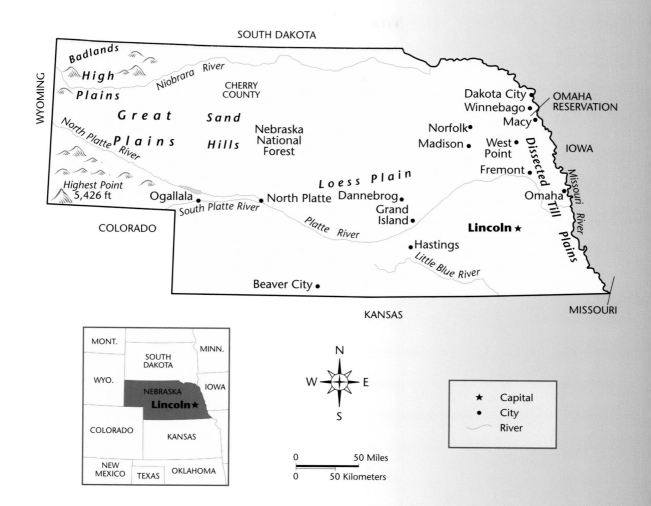

SOUTH DAKOTA

Badlands

High

Plains

Niobrara River

WYOMING

CHERRY
COUNTY

Great

Sand

Plains

Hills

Nebraska
National
Forest

North Platte River

Highest Point
5,426 ft

Ogallala •

South Platte River

COLORADO

North Platte

Loess Plain

Dannebrog •

Platte River

Grand
Island •

Dakota City •

Winnebago •

OMAHA
RESERVATION

Macy

Norfolk•

Madison •

West
Point

IOWA

Fremont •

Omaha

Dissected Till Plains

Missouri River

Lincoln ★

• Hastings

Little Blue River

Beaver City •

KANSAS

MISSOURI

MONT.

SOUTH
DAKOTA

MINN.

WYO.

NEBRASKA

Lincoln ★

IOWA

COLORADO

KANSAS

NEW
MEXICO

TEXAS

OKLAHOMA

N

W   E

S

0   50 Miles
0   50 Kilometers

★   Capital
•   City
      River

Glossary

abolition   the termination of slavery in the United States

advocate   a person who argues for, or defends, a cause

amend   to change

aquifer   a layer of rock that releases water

aviary   a large enclosure for confining birds

bill   draft of a proposed law presented to a legislative body for approval

bone marrow   the soft material made up of fat cells and blood cells that fills bone cavities

botany   the study of plants

capital   a city that is the official seat of government in a state

capitol   a building in which a state legislature assembles

Civil War   the war between the states in the North and South United States from 1861 to 1865

continental   part of the 48 contiguous (neighboring, or sharing a boundary) states in the United States

dean   officer of a college or university

Democrat   a member of the Democratic Party, one of two major political parties in the United States

Emmy award   award issued by the Academy of Television Arts and Sciences for achievement in television

epilepsy   an illness causing episodes of body spasms or seizures

eroded   worn away by constant contact with water or wind

excavation   the action of exposing or uncovering by digging

expedition   an organized group of people taking a journey

fawns   baby deer

fertile   rich in material needed to sustain plant growth

fossil   remnant, such as a skeleton, of an organism from a past geologic age

glacier   a large, slow moving mass of ice

Great Depression   a period of severe economic hardship during the 1930s

Homestead Act   1862 Act passed by the U.S. Congress which gave 160 acres of land to any free man

immigrants   people who leave one country to settle permanently in another

industry   the manufacturing and sale of products

irrigate   to supply water to land using ditches, pipes, or streams

living history museum   a museum with actors who dress in costumes of a particular era and portray workers and townspeople

mammoth   prehistoric elephant-like mammal

Missouri Compromise   1820 Act passed by the U.S. Congress that banned slavery north of Missouri

native originally living or growing in a certain place

nonpartisan not promoting separate political parties

perennial growing or recurring every year

pioneer one who ventures into unknown territory to settle

Pulitzer Prize award established by Joseph Pulitzer for accomplishment in journalism, literature, and music

reservations tracts of land set apart by the government for special use

scout one who explores and gathers information

slavery the state of a person who is bound to provide service to a master or household

stroboscope an instrument used to view and balance moving objects by making them appear stationary

temperate neither hot nor cold

till rich soil made up of sand, clay, and gravel left by glaciers

transcontinental crossing a continent

veto to prevent from becoming law

World War I a war fought from 1914 to 1918 in which the United States, Great Britain, France, the Soviet Union, and other allies defeated Germany, Austria-Hungary, Turkey, and Bulgaria

World War II a war fought from 1939 to 1945 in which the United States, Great Britain, France, the Soviet Union, and other allies defeated Germany, Italy, and Japan

More Books to Read

Bueckner, Thomas R. *Fort Robinson and the American West, 1874–1899.* Norman: University of Oklahoma Press, 2003.

Clark, LaVerne Harrell. *Mari Sandoz's Native Nebraska.* Charleston, SC: Arcadia Press, 2001.

McNally, Hanna. *Nebraska: Off the Beaten Path.* 4th ed. Guilford, Conn.: Globe Pequot Press, 2003.

Naugle, Ronald C., and Erastus Flavel Beadle. *Ham, Eggs and Corn Cake: A Nebraska Territory Diary.* Lincoln: University of Nebraska Press, 2001.

Weatherly, Myra S., Melissa N. Matusevich, and Karen Wyatt Drevo. *Nebraska (From Sea to Shining Sea).* Minneapolis, MN: Children's Press, 2003.

Index

About the Author

Jamie Stockman Opat is a writer with twelve years of experience in public relations and journalism. She grew up on a farm near Kirwin, Kansas, close to the Nebraska border. She currently lives in Wichita, Kansas, with her husband and son.